23.2

Science STARTS

A+ books

MAGNETS PUSH, MAGNETS PULL

by Mark Weakland

CAPSTONE PRESS
a capstone imprint

Have you ever held two magnets close together?

2

Like magic, magnets pull together and push apart. What gives magnets their strange strength?

Magnets are made from metals.

Some magnets, called lodestones, are found in the earth.

lodestones

Made of iron ore magnetite, lodestones are natural magnets.

Natural magnets are hard to find. But one lodestone can make many more magnets.

6

When a lodestone is rubbed against another metal, it creates a new magnet.

Like a bubble, magnetic energy surrounds a magnet.

To see a magnet's energy, sprinkle powdered iron around it.

The iron powder follows a magnet's lines of energy.

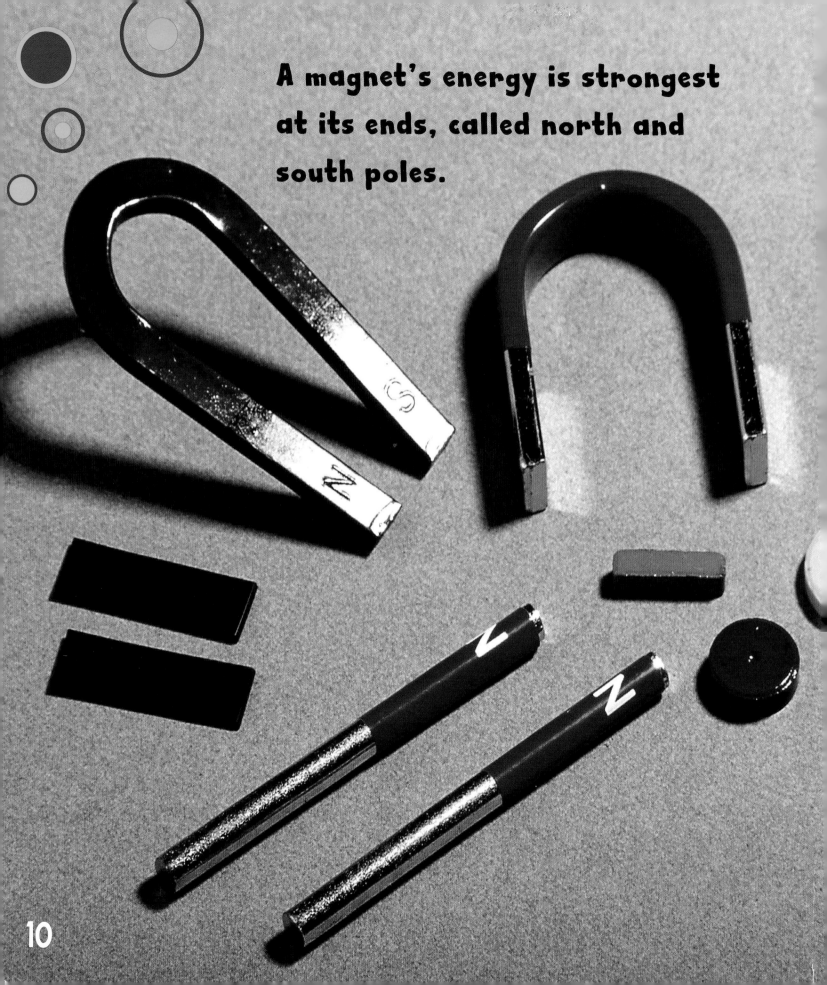

A magnet's energy is strongest at its ends, called north and south poles.

The Earth produces magnetic energy, just like a magnet.

north pole

south pole

And like a magnet, the Earth has a magnetic north and south pole.

Poles that are opposite attract each other. All magnets attract objects made with iron.

Nails and paper clips stick to a magnet because they contain iron. So do cars, stoves, and refrigerators.

Two poles that are the same push each other away. Magnets can also repel metal. A metal ring floats above a magnet. The invisible force of magnetic energy pushes the ring up and away.

Where are magnets found? Everywhere! At the airport, magnets keep planes from getting flat tires.

A rolling magnetic sweeper picks up all stray metal to keep tires safe.

A small electric motor
powers this toy train. Inside
the motor are tiny magnets.
Magnets also turn the steel
wheels of a diesel locomotive.

18

Electric motors,
big and small,
use magnets.

Electric motors
are everywhere.

Without magnets and electric motors, there would be no spinning fans and no whirling beaters on a cake mixer.

Magnets have many other uses. To make his music louder, a guitarist uses an amplifier. The speakers in an amplifier use magnets to make sound.

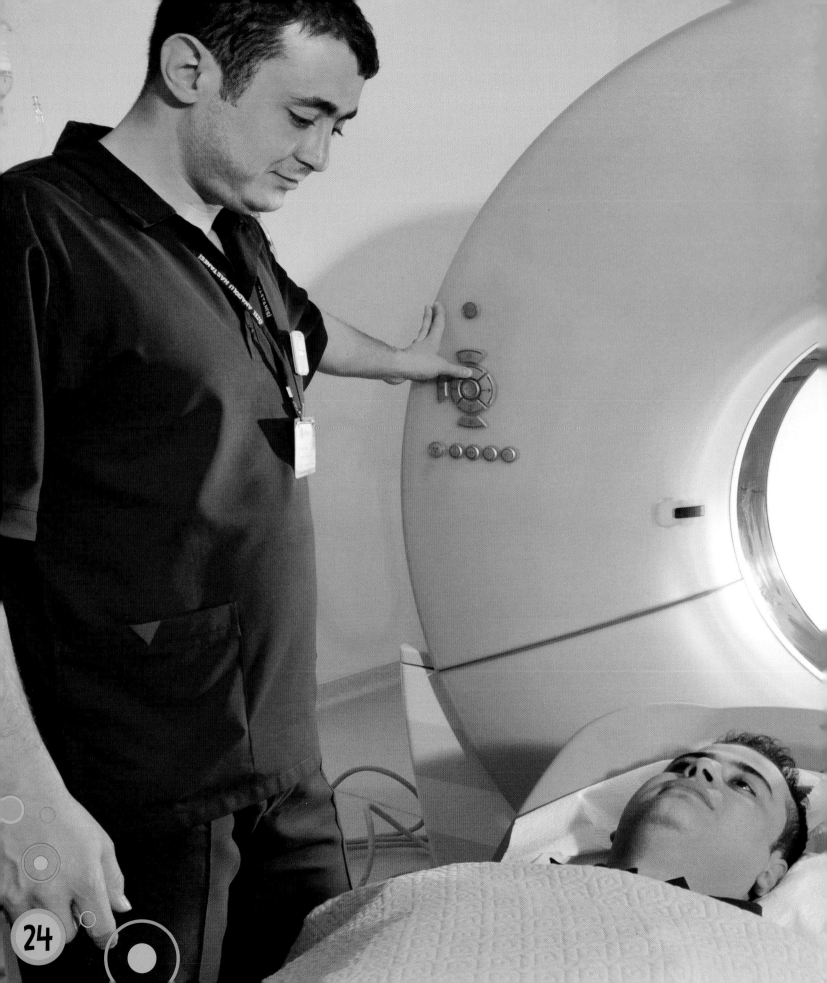

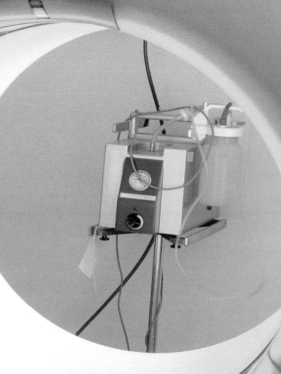

In a hospital, a patient slowly slides into the center of a large ring magnet.

Doctors use the MRI machine to find out why a person is sick.

25

A magnet can move the heaviest objects. Some magnets are strong enough to lift more than 2,000 pounds (907 kilograms)!

With magnets shaped like letters, you can spell words and send messages. What do these magnets spell?

Glossary

amplifier—a piece of equipment that makes sound louder

attract—to pull together

iron—a very hard metal

lodestone—a hard, black rock found in earth that attracts iron

pole—one of the two ends of a magnet; a pole can also be the top or bottom part of a planet

repel—to push apart

Read More

Boothroyd, Jennifer. *Attract and Repel: A Look at Magnets*. Exploring Physical Science. Minneapolis: Lerner Publications, 2011.

Higgins, Nadia. *Mighty Magnets*. Science Rocks! Edina, Minn.: Magic Wagon, 2009.

Royston, Angela. *Magnets*. My World of Science. Chicago: Heinemann Library, 2008.

Internet Sites

FactHound offers a safe, fun way to find Internet sites related to this book. All of the sites on FactHound have been researched by our staff.

Here's all you do:

Visit *www.facthound.com*

Type in this code: 9781429652513

 **Super-cool stuff!** Check out projects, games and lots more at **www.capstonekids.com**

Index

A+ Books are published by Capstone Press,
151 Good Counsel Drive, P.O. Box 669,
Mankato, Minnesota 56002.
www.capstonepub.com

 Books published by Capstone Press are manufactured with paper
containing at least 10 percent post-consumer waste.

Library of Congress Cataloging-in-Publication Data
Weakland, Mark.
   Magnets push, magnets pull / by Mark Weakland.
      p. cm.—(A+ books. Science starts)
   Includes bibliographical references and index.
      ISBN 978-1-4296-5251-3 (library binding)—ISBN 978-1-4296-6147-8 (paperback)
         1. Magnets—Juvenile literature. 2. Magnetism—Juvenile literature. I. Title.
      QC757.5.W43 2011
         538'.4—dc22   2010038879

Credits

Jenny Marks, editor; Alison Thiele, designer; Marcie Spence, media researcher; Eric Manske, production specialist

Photo Credits

Capstone Studio: Karon Dubke, 28–29; Getty Images Inc.: Amy Coopes/AFP, 4–5, DEA/Photo 1/De Agostini, 6–7; iStockphoto: drnadig, 18–19, philipdyer, 22–23, Tommounsey, 1, 8-9; PhotoEdit Inc.: Bill Aron, 2–3, Tony Freeman, 10; Photo Researchers, Inc.: John R. Foster, 14–15; Shutterstock: Denis Tabler, 11, Dmitriy Yakovlev, 20, iofoto, cover, Levent Konuk, 24–25, Matt Antonino, 21, Pefkos, 12–13; Storch Magnetics: 16–17; Visuals Unlimited: Marli Miller, 26–27

Note to Parents, Teachers, and Librarians

The Science Starts series supports national education standards related to science. This book describes and illustrates magnets. The images support early readers in understanding the text. The repetition of words and phrases helps early readers learn new words. This book also introduces early readers to subject-specific vocabulary words, which are defined in the Glossary section. Early readers may need assistance to read some words and to use the Glossary, Read More, Internet Sites, and Index sections of the book.

Printed in the United States of America in North Mankato, Minnesota.
092010   005933CGS11